Finding a Home

Building Bridges Series

Gate
HOUSE

Building Bridges Series: Finding a Home
Text by Catherine White
Illustrations by Marta Kwasniewska
Copyright © Gatehouse Media Limited 2017

First published and distributed in 2017 by Gatehouse Media Limited

ISBN: 978-1-84231-174-5

British Library Cataloguing-in-Publication Data:
A catalogue record for this book is available from the British Library

Jamal lives with his friend, Dan.

Dan owns a house.

Jamal rents a room in the house.

Jamal has lived with Dan for two years.

Jamal has lived with Dan
since he first came to England.

Now Dan is getting married.

He is getting married to Meg, his girlfriend.

Dan and Meg want to live alone.

They want to start a family.

Jamal must find somewhere else to live.
He must look for a place of his own.

Jamal looks at the small ads
in the local newspaper.
He looks at the notices in the window
of the corner shop.
He looks in the local estate agent's window.
He looks online at the property websites.
He looks everywhere.

Jamal wants a one bedroom flat
with a living room, kitchen and bathroom.
Jamal doesn't have any furniture,
so a furnished flat would be best for him.

Jamal wants to live near his college.

He wants to live near his friends.

He wants to live near the shops
and on a bus route into town.

The rents are high.
Flats are very expensive.
Perhaps he will have to share a flat
with someone else.
Perhaps he will just find a room
to rent instead.

That will be much cheaper, Jamal thinks.

Jamal asks everyone at college.
Sally tells Jamal that her brother
has a spare room in his house.

"He needs some extra money," she says.
"I'll ask him if he'll rent it to you."

Sally goes to see her brother, Pete.
She tells Pete all about her friend, Jamal.

Jamal sounds like someone I could get on well with, Pete thinks. *And I could really do with the extra money.*

"It's not a bad idea," Pete says.
"Let's meet up and have a talk about it."

Sally arranges for Pete to meet Jamal.
Pete and Jamal like each other.
They seem to have a lot in common.
They both think it might work out.

"OK, let's give it a go," says Pete.
"When can you move in?"

"Tomorrow," Jamal says, "I can move in
tomorrow."
Jamal smiles.
He is happy he has found a new place to live.

Gatehouse Books®

Gatehouse Books are written for older teenagers and adults who are developing their basic reading and writing or English language skills.

The format of our books is clear and uncluttered.
The language is familiar and the text is often line-broken, so that each line ends at a natural pause.

Gatehouse Books are widely used within Adult Basic Education throughout the English speaking world.
They are also a valuable resource within the Prison Education Service and Probation Services, Social Services and secondary schools - in both basic skills and ESOL teaching.

Catalogue available

Gatehouse Media Limited
PO Box 965
Warrington
WA4 9DE

Tel/Fax: 01925 267778
E-mail: info@gatehousebooks.com
Website: www.gatehousebooks.com

KING ST.

Set Three
BOOK 7

Steve Gets a Job

Steve Gets a Job
King Street: Readers Set Three - Book 7
Copyright © Iris Nunn 2014

Text: Iris Nunn
Editor: June Lewis

Published in 2014 by Gatehouse Media Limited

ISBN: 978-1-84231-132-5

British Library Cataloguing-in-Publication Data:
A catalogue record for this book is available from the British Library

You have met Steve.
He is a student.
He is an art student.

He lives in a house with Ros
and Sally.
They are students.
They have jobs.
Sally babysits.
Ros helps in the shop.

Steve would like a job.
He needs the money.

"What can I do?"
he asks Sally one day.

"Think about what you are good at,"
says Sally.

"Well, I am a good cook.
I can make baked potatoes.
I can make a sandwich.
I can make beefburgers and chips.
I can make egg and chips."

"And beans and chips!" says Sally.
"Look, at the pub that is what you get:
sandwiches, baked potatoes, chips.
Go to the pub and ask Sid for a job."

Steve thinks, "I might as well.
Sid can say yes or he can say no.
If I want a job I have to ask."

Steve goes to the pub on a Thursday
to play darts.

This week he goes on Monday.
Sid is in the bar.
It is very quiet.

"Have you come
for a game of darts?"
asks Sid.

"No, Sid. I want a job.
Can you help me?"

"I could do with some help
in the kitchen on Friday nights.
Brenda likes to go to see Jenny
on a Friday.
She comes back late.
Can you cook?"

"I can. I would like to cook for you,"
says Steve. "Friday is fine."

"Come in this evening
and watch Brenda in the kitchen.
She will show you what to do.
You can have a try.
Three hours on Friday evenings,
starting this Friday."

Steve went to the pub in the evening
to see Brenda.
Brenda showed him what to do.

She showed him
where everything was.

She showed him
how she made sandwiches.

She showed him
how she made baked potatoes.

She showed him
how she made the chips,
the beans, the eggs
and the beefburgers.

And she showed him
how to take the pasta bake
out of the freezer.

"You can give me a hand on Friday, Steve, and I can see if you will cope."

On Friday Steve went to the pub
at six o'clock.
Brenda was making a sandwich
for a customer,
a ham sandwich.

"Steve, can you pop a potato
in the microwave?"

Steve helped Brenda till nine o'clock.
He had coped very well,
but he was tired.

And what did Brenda think?

"Steve, you will do!"